MICKEY'S PRACTICE WORKBOOKS

READING COMPREHENSION

ISBN: 0-448-16123-0
Copyright © MCMLXXVIII Walt Disney Productions.
World Wide Rights Reserved.
Printed in the United States of America
Published simultaneously in Canada

Published by WONDER BOOKS

A Division of Grosset & Dunlap
A Filmways Company
Publishers • New York

Note to Parents

Use the fun stories, poems, activities, and games in this book to help your youngsters build reading skills and increase reading comprehension. Check the activity pages as your children complete them. To give your children a real sense of accomplishment, draw a smiling face on each page they complete. And **do** give help whenever asked. Too-busy parents can frequently discourage children from learning!

Most of all, enjoy this book together. You will be helping your children to learn and want to learn. You will be helping them to develop skills that can be the foundations for a successful life. And you will be doing it together.

Contents

The Word Fairy Says:

These words are listed in the order of introduction, rather than alphabetically. Your children should know these words, but might find them new to their reading vocabulary. Give help when needed.

swimming	squealed	UFO	sidewalks
dinosaur	pizza	captain	mustard
cheesecake	whispered	sneezed	squirted
poked	growled	grumped	sprayed
scat	nibble	answer	scissors
copycat	yawned	bashful	parrot
kangaroo	chattered	dwarfs	collar
cricket	flapped	puddled	Mexican
umbrella	wiggle	hissing	jumping beans
shy	uncle	excitement	crocodile
twinkling	skateboard	squeezing	bookends
telescope	problem	rowing	mischief

What Does Donald Do?

What does Donald do at night?
I never hear his "quack."
I wonder if he goes to sleep
On tummy, side, or back?

Circle the way **you** think Donald sleeps at night.

Donald Is a Lucky Duck!

Donald was swimming in the pond. He was happy. It was a warm day and the pond felt good.

Suddenly Donald saw Mickey near the pond. Mickey was hot and tired. The cool pond looked good to Mickey. He wanted to swim, too!

Mickey held his nose. Then he jumped into the pond. Splash! Mickey was in the water. But he forgot he couldn't swim!

"Take my hand," called Donald Duck. "I'll help you."

Mickey held onto Donald's hand. "Thank you, Donald," he said. " You are a good mouse-saver. You're a lucky duck!"

Donald laughed. He was happy to help Mickey. "But," said Donald, "don't jump in again until you learn how to swim. You may not find a lucky duck again!"

Now Do This!

(Circle) the sentence that tells something about Donald Duck.

Donald is a lucky duck.

Donald is a dinosaur.

Mickey was hot and tired.

Donald is a good mouse-saver.

Write 1, 2, or 3 to put the sentences in the right order.

_____ "You are a good mouse-saver."

_____ Mickey jumped into the pond.

_____ Donald was swimming in the pond.

7

Who Doesn't Like Cheese?

Mickey is a mouse. His friend Minnie is a mouse, too. People say they are alike. Mickey has big ears. So does Minnie. Mickey has a long, thin tail. So does Minnie Mouse.

But Mickey and Minnie are different, too. Minnie has long eyelashes. Mickey doesn't. Minnie wears a skirt. Mickey doesn't.

Minnie likes all kinds of cheese. Mickey doesn't. But, guess what! There's one cheese they both like. They both like cheesecake! And guess who makes the cheesecake that they both eat? If you guessed Minnie Mouse, you are wrong. Mickey is the best cheesecake baker in the whole mouse world!

Now Do This!

(Circle) the sentence

that tells something about the story.

Minnie has big ears.

Mickey and Minnie have long tails.

Mickey likes to play ball.

Mickey chases cats.

Mickey is the best cheesecake baker.

(Circle) the word that best finishes each sentence.
Then write the word.

Mickey has big _____

Minnie has a long _____

Mickey bakes _____

Mickey and Minnie are _____

Scat, Cat!

"Look at Cleo," said Lucifer to himself. "She looks fat. And I'm hungry." Lucifer looked at Cleo. Cleo looked at Lucifer.

The cat walked around the fishbowl looking at Cleo. Then Lucifer put his paw into the water.

But Cleo just swam away. Now Lucifer was getting very hungry. He wanted a fish dinner. He was getting angry, too. And Lucifer couldn't wait for his dinner.

So Lucifer put his paw into the fishbowl again. He tried to grab Cleo!

Cleo didn't want to be his dinner. She swam up to the top of the bowl. She took a big gulp of water. She stuck her head out of the bowl. A stream of water went right toward Lucifer's eye. That was Cleo's way of saying, "Scat, cat!"

Lucifer was so surprised, he ran away. And that was the end of his fish dinner. He really did **scat!**

Now Do This!

Circle the sentence that tells something about the story.

Cleo is a fat fish.

Lucifer is a hungry cat.

Cleo wanted a fish dinner.

Lucifer shouted, "Scat, cat!"

Lucifer had a fish dinner.

Lucifer ran away.

Write 1, 2, or 3 to put the sentences in the right order.

_2_ Cleo stuck her head out of the bowl.
_1_ Lucifer looked at Cleo.
_3_ Lucifer ran away.

Draw a picture of Cleo laughing at Lucifer.

My Shadow

I have a little copycat
Who follows me all day,
Going everywhere I go,
Playing where I play.

But when the sun has gone to bed,
And dark is all around,
I cannot see my copycat—
He's nowhere to be found!

Now Do This!

Finish my shadow. Color it.

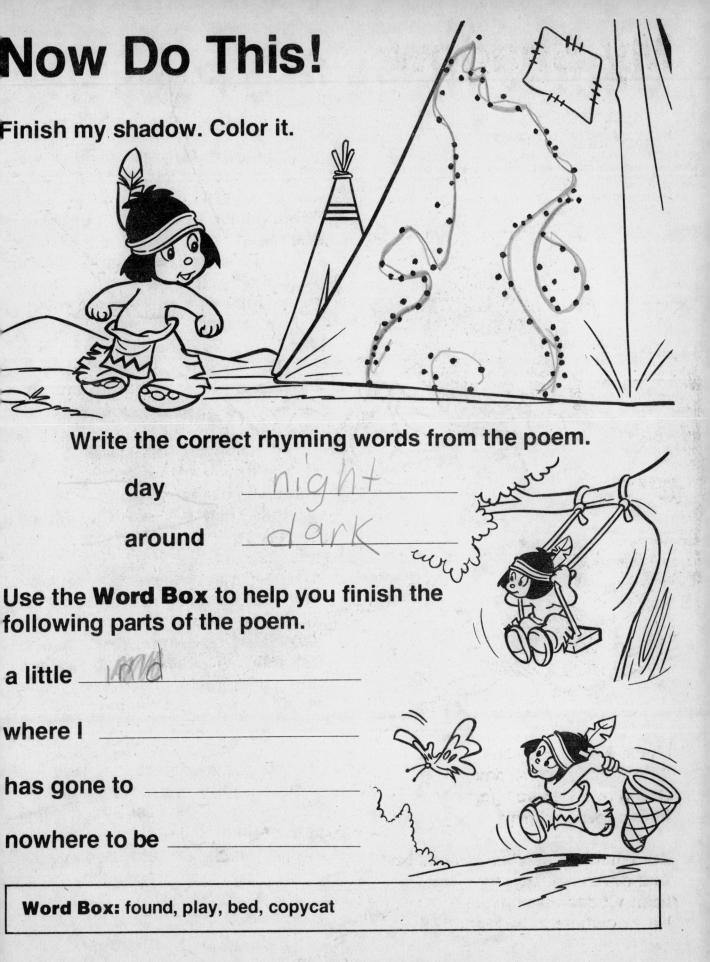

Write the correct rhyming words from the poem.

day   _night_

around   _dark_

Use the Word Box to help you finish the following parts of the poem.

a little _____

where I _____

has gone to _____

nowhere to be _____

Word Box: found, play, bed, copycat

13

Jiminy Rides in a Pocket!

Jiminy Cricket was out for a walk. But he had walked farther than he meant to walk. Now he was hot and tired. Jiminy sat down by the side of the road to rest.

Suddenly he heard someone coming. Jiminy stood up. "Hi," he said. "I'm Jiminy Cricket. Who are you?"

"I'm Kanga," answered the shy kangaroo. "And this is my baby, Roo."

"Glad to meet you," said Jiminy, and he tipped his hat. "I'm so tired. I've walked too far today. And it's a long way back."

"I'll help you," said Kanga. "Just climb into my pocket with Roo. I'll get you back. I'm not tired."

Jiminy had a great ride. Kanga's pocket was just the thing for the tired cricket.

When the ride was over, Jiminy thanked Kanga. "You've been very kind," he said. "Now I'd like to do something for you. Here, take my umbrella. When it rains, you can hold it over your baby, and Roo won't get wet at all."

Kanga smiled shyly and took the umbrella. She tucked it into her pocket and hopped on her way.

Now, when you see Kanga and Roo on rainy days, you always see them using Jiminy's umbrella. And Jiminy always remembers his ride in a pocket!

Now Do This!

(Circle) words used in Jiminy's story.

walk	tired	umbrella	ride
hot	Kanga	roof	summer
cold	dinner	pocket	baby

(Circle) the sentence that tells something about the story.

Jiminy was hot and tired.

Kanga was taking a nap.

Roo was in Kanga's pocket.

Jiminy rode in Kanga's pocket.

Kanga gave Jiminy an umbrella.

15

What Was in the Sky?

"Just look at those stars," said Dad. "They're really twinkling and winking tonight!"

"Let me look," said John.

Dad started to give John the telescope. Suddenly he shouted, "Wait! Wait a minute. I see something different. It looks like a ship—a flying ship in the sky! Quick, take a look. Maybe it's a UFO!"

"A UFO?" asked John as he took the telescope. "You mean an Unidentified Flying Object? Something from outer space? Wow! Let me look."

John was shaking. He didn't know whether UFOs were real or not. But he had heard a lot about them.

John put the telescope to his eye. He looked up into the sky. He did see something. And it **was** a ship—a ship with sails! The ship was sparkling. John looked harder. He could just

see the captain of the ship. He was all dressed in green. And then he saw something in a tiny ball of light near the captain.

John smiled. Now he knew what the flying ship was. He knew who the captain was. And he knew what the tiny ball of light was. As he looked, the flying ship floated away.

"Well, John," said Dad. "Did you see it? Did you see the flying ship?"

"I didn't see a thing, Dad," said John. "I guess your eyes were playing tricks on you. Let's go in now."

"Dad would never believe me," thought John as they went into the house. But John knew he had seen Peter Pan's flying ship. And he had seen Peter, himself—and Tinker Bell, too.

John was so glad to know that they were still up there. Aren't you?

Now Do This!

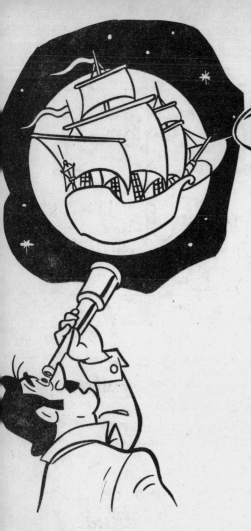

Circle a word that could be used in place of the underlined word in each sentence.

1. **The stars were twinkling.**

   shining   shooting   talking

2. **Dad thought he saw a flying ship.**

   shoe   boat   star

3. **John was shaking.**

   eating   smiling   shivering

4. **John and Dad went into the house.**

   home   car   ship

Print T for True and F for False beside each sentence.

Dad was using a telescope. _____

John was on a flying ship. _____

John saw Peter Pan and Tinker Bell. _____

Dad knew what John saw. _____

Read and Color

Color Jiminy Cricket's hat  **green.**

Color Sleeping Beauty's dress  **pink.**

Color the Ugly Duckling  **yellow.**

Color Babe, the ox **blue.**

Color Tigger  **orange.**

Color Tramp a coat of  **brown.**

Color the Queen of Hearts  **red.**

Read and Do

(Circle) the word that best finishes each sentence. Then write the word.

Donald is in his **bed** book

Dumbo has big tears **ears**

Kanga baked a rake **cake**

Cinderella needs a **slipper** dipper

Pinocchio's nose **grew** flew

Grumpy is always **sad** mad

Pluto is a **dog** frog

Gus is a house **mouse**

20

Seven Surprises for Snow White

The Seven Dwarfs wanted to make Snow White happy. They wanted her to stay and stay. But she had so much work to do each day.

"Let's surprise Snow White," said Doc. "We'll choose jobs to do each day. That will make Snow White happy."

Sneezy sneezed and Grumpy grumped. But they all agreed to help surprise her.

"I'll make the beds," said Sleepy. "I like beds best of all."

"I'll cook the food," said Sneezy. "But I won't use any pepper. Pepper makes me sneeze."

"I'll answer the door when someone knocks," said Bashful. "Then maybe I won't be so bashful any more."

"I'll whistle while I wash the floors," said Happy. "You know I like to whistle."

"Dopey, you bring in the wood for the fire," said Doc. "And I'll wash the dishes."

But Grumpy didn't say anything. The six other dwarfs looked at Grumpy. They waited for him to tell what he would do.

At last Grumpy spoke. "I won't grump ever again," he said. "Well, at least hardly ever. And that will **really** surprise Snow White!"

The dwarfs did all the things they said. They really did surprise Snow White. She was so pleased, she baked three cherry pies. And they had a party that very night.

Now Do This!

Circle each word that tells about one of the dwarfs.

happy	sleepy	doc	sunny
grumpy	goofy	fairy	sneezy
itchy	bashful	dopey	baby

Circle a sentence that tells something about the story.

The dwarfs wanted to help Snow White.

Sleepy wanted to make the beds.

Sneezy wanted to use pepper.

Snow White met Prince Charming.

Snow White was happy.

The Friendly Snake

A friendly snake went walking
On a puddled garden path,
And there he saw a duckling
At his early morning bath.

The snake spoke to the duckling
In his hissing snakelike way.
The little duck said, "Quack, quack, quack!"
And quickly ran away!

The friendly snake was puzzled
By the duckling and its quack,
For all the snake had asked was,
"Can I help you wash your back?"

Now Do This!

(Circle) each word that is used in the poem.

friendly

bird

duckling

bath

book

little

girl

worm

snake

back

bubbles

house

garden

flew

**Follow the dots. Begin at A and go to Z.
Then color the picture you've made.**

Who Fell Off the Skateboard?

Huey, Dewey, and Louie had a problem. There were three of them and only one uncle.

"I want Uncle Donald to go to the circus with me," said Huey. "We can laugh at the clowns and eat popcorn."

"I want Uncle Donald to go to the zoo with me," said Dewey. "We can feed the baby animals."

"I want Uncle Donald to take me to the park," said Louie. "I haven't used my new skateboard yet."

"Pipe down, you three!" said Donald. "I'll tell you what we'll do. We'll follow the alphabet. First, I'll go to the zoo with D for Dewey. Then I'll go to the circus with H for Huey. And then I'll go to the park with L for Louie."

And so he did! But guess who lost his hat . . .

ate too much popcorn . . .

and fell off the skateboard?

Uncle Donald, that's who!

Now Do This!

Write the numbers 1 to 4 to put the pictures in the right order

(Circle) a sentence that tells something about the story.

The three ducks had a problem.

Huey wanted to go to the park.

Dewey wanted to go to the zoo.

Louie ate too much popcorn.

Donald fell off the skateboard.

Donald is an uncle.

Circle the words that rhyme with quack.

pack	tack	peek
book	cake	lack
sack	back	skate

One Left Shoe

I know some things
That come in twos,
Like eyes and ears
And socks and shoes.

And two best friends
Are company,
But it's a crowd
If there are three.

But there are times
When one will do,
Like one long nose
And one left shoe!

Now Do This!

Draw lines to match the pictures to the names.

Bernard and Bianca

Baloo

Dumbo

Chip and Dale

Lady and Tramp

Big Bad Wolf

Pongo and Perdita

Mickey and Minnie

Read and Finish!

Use the words from the **Word Fairy's Box** to help you finish each sentence.

Uncle Scrooge is the world's richest _____

Cinderella had a fairy _____

The Cheshire Cat has a big _____

Alice followed a white _____

The Ugly Duckling was a _____

Snow White is a beautiful _____

Geppetto's pet is a _____ called Cleo.

Bambi is a baby _____

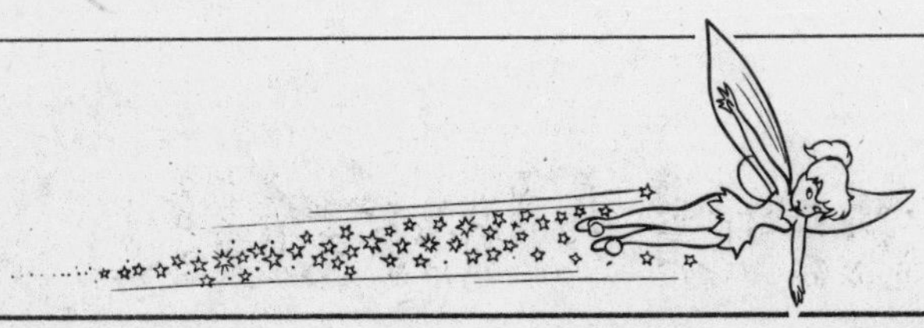

Word Fairy's Box:

duck, rabbit, swan, godmother, princess, deer, goldfish, grin

31

Who Ate the Pizza?

"I'm hungry," said the Big Bad Wolf. "I'm so hungry I could eat three pigs!"

"We're not good to eat right now," squealed the Three Little Pigs. "We're not fat enough yet."

"Eat a big dinner," said the wolf. "And then you can be **my** dinner!" And he rubbed his hands together.

But the Three Little Pigs were smart. "Let's cook pizza," they whispered. And they did.

The pizza smelled good to the wolf. "I'll eat some of that before I eat you," he growled.

The wolf began to eat the pizza. And he began to drink a lot of water because the pizza was very hot.

Before he knew it, the pizza was all gone. So was the water. And the Big Bad Wolf's tummy was as fat as it could be. The Big Bad Wolf was full. He could not eat another thing, not even a pig. And he fell sound asleep.

The Three Little Pigs laughed. And they danced and sang their good song all the way home: "Who's afraid of the big bad wolf, the big bad wolf, the big bad wolf? Tra-la-la-la-la!"

Now Do This!

Circle two words that help to finish each sentence. Then complete the sentence.

1. "I'm hungry," said the Big _____.

   Bad   sad   Wolf

2. The pizza _____.

   wolf   good   smelled

3. "I could eat _____."

   four   pigs   three

4. The wolf fell _____.

   sound   awake   asleep

Circle the sentence that tells something about the story.

The Big Bad Wolf was hungry.

The Three Pigs made pizza.

The Big Bad Wolf drank water.

The pigs ate the pizza.

The Big Bad Wolf fell asleep.

The wolf sang and danced.

The Fangaroo Bopped!

There was a kunny fangaroo—
I mean a funny kangaroo
Who tried to do a hunny bop—
I mean he tried a bunny hop,
But all he did was belly-flop
Because his feet went floppety-flip,
Instead of going hoppety-hip—
I mean, instead of hippety-hop—
Oh, well—I guess
The fangaroo bopped!

Circle all the made-up words used in the poem.

kunny	fangaroo	funny	bopped
kangaroo	hopped	hunny	feet

Bambi Saves Thumper

It was cold in the forest. The wind was blowing little snowflakes all around. Soon it would be dark. Bambi was having a last nibble on some tender branches before going to sleep.

"H-h-h-h-elp me!" Bambi heard. "Help me, please!"

It was Thumper, the rabbit. Bambi knew Thumper's voice very well.

"What's wrong, Thumper?" asked Bambi. "How can I help you? What can I do?"

"I'm sick," chattered the rabbit. "I ate some berries that were not good. Now I have a tummyache, and I'm sh-sh-shivering."

"Curl up close to me," said the deer.

"I'll keep you warm and safe." And Bambi lay down on the cold ground.

All night long Bambi stayed awake and took care of Thumper. He kept the little rabbit warm and safe from the cold wind and snow. Thumper slept and slept.

When morning came, Thumper woke up. His tummyache was gone. He felt better.

"Thank you, Bambi," said Thumper. "You really are a good forest friend. You saved my life." And he ran away to find some good food to eat.

Bambi yawned and stretched. He was tired from being awake all night. But at least his friend was safe. Now he could sleep. His long night was over.

Now Do This!

Write the answer to each question.

What was Bambi nibbling? _____

Who was sick? _____

What did Thumper eat? _____

What did Thumper have? _____

Who helped save Thumper? _____

⟨Circle⟩ the words from the story about Bambi and Thumper.

forest	cheese	sick
snowflakes	shivering	silly
summer	shells	friend
chipmunk	deer	fun
checkers	dinosaur	night

Read the S-Map

Use the map and the map key to answer the questions.

S-Town

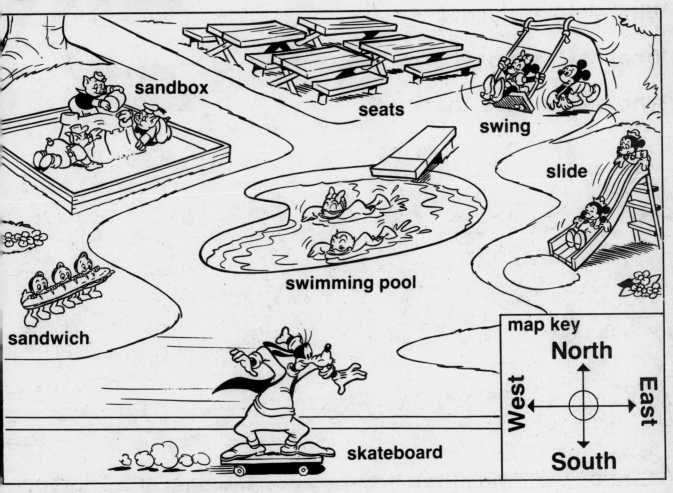

sandbox

seats

swing

slide

swimming pool

sandwich

skateboard

map key

North

West

East

South

1. If you were at the swimming pool, would you go north or south to the swing? _____

2. Where would you go to the skateboard? _____

3. Where would you go to eat? _____

4. Where would you go to the slide? _____

5. Where would you go to sit? _____

Pick a Poem

Clown Faces

Do you ever wonder,
When you see a clown
Whose face is painted glad,
That maybe underneath the paint
The clown is really sad?

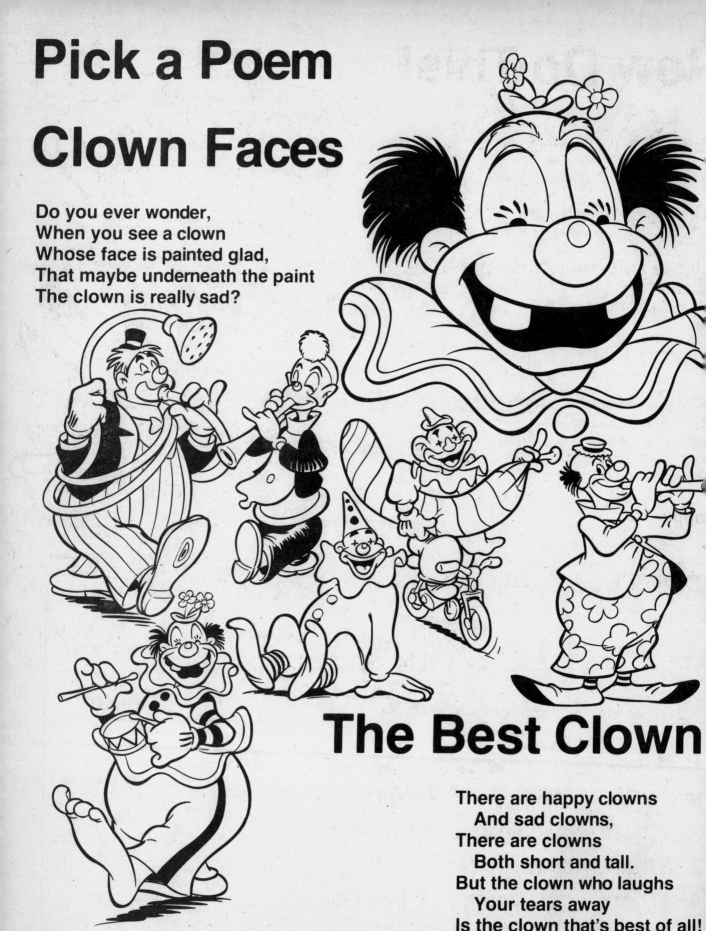

The Best Clown

There are happy clowns
   And sad clowns,
There are clowns
   Both short and tall.
But the clown who laughs
   Your tears away
Is the clown that's best of all!

Now Do This!

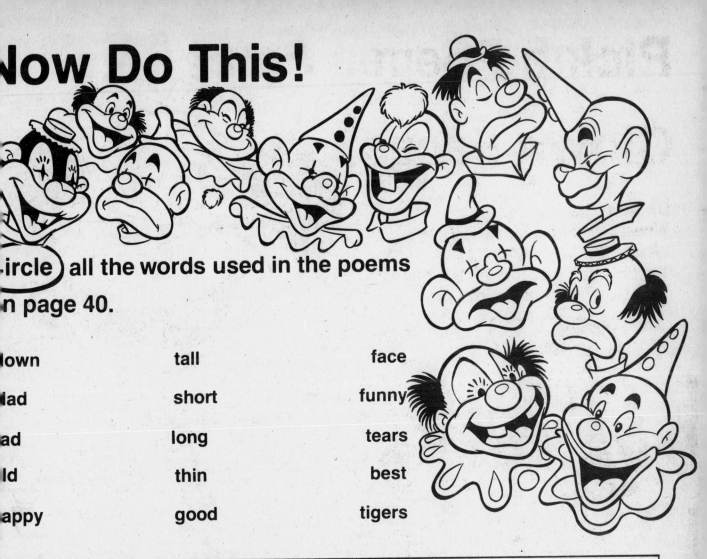

ircle all the words used in the poems
n page 40.

lown	tall	face
Nad	short	funny
ad	long	tears
ld	thin	best
appy	good	tigers

Draw a picture of the clown you like the best.

Dumbo Saves Peter Pan

Peter Pan was flying up over the circus. He was watching all the animal acts down below. It was fun seeing the circus from the air.

Suddenly, Peter felt himself falling. He moved his arms. Nothing happened. He couldn't fly any more. He was falling slowly down.

"Help, help!" cried Peter Pan. "Somebody, please help me! I'm falling!"

Dumbo heard Peter. He looked up and saw Peter falling down from the sky. Dumbo flapped his big ears. Up, up, he went as fast as he could go.

"I'm coming, Peter," called Dumbo. "I'm coming to help you."

Dumbo flew under Peter Pan. Peter

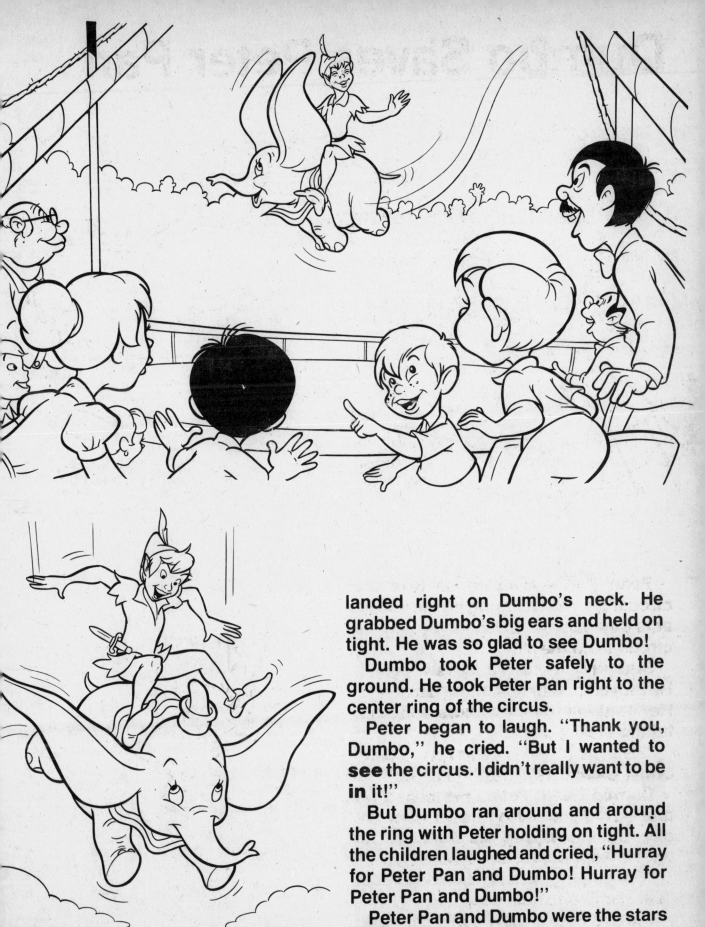

landed right on Dumbo's neck. He grabbed Dumbo's big ears and held on tight. He was so glad to see Dumbo!

Dumbo took Peter safely to the ground. He took Peter Pan right to the center ring of the circus.

Peter began to laugh. "Thank you, Dumbo," he cried. "But I wanted to **see** the circus. I didn't really want to be **in** it!"

But Dumbo ran around and around the ring with Peter holding on tight. All the children laughed and cried, "Hurray for Peter Pan and Dumbo! Hurray for Peter Pan and Dumbo!"

Peter Pan and Dumbo were the stars of the big circus that day!

Now Do This!

Print T for True or F for False beside each sentence.

Peter couldn't fly any more. _____

A clown heard Peter cry for help. _____

Peter landed on Dumbo's neck. _____

Peter took part in the circus. _____

Dumbo saved Peter Pan. _____

(Circle) Yes or No for each question.

1. Could Peter Pan fly at first?   yes   no

2. Was Peter flying over a circus?   yes   no

3. Was Tinker Bell with Peter?   yes   no

4. Did Peter Pan start to fall?   yes   no

5. Did Wendy help Peter Pan?   yes   no

The Circus

I always go the circus
To look, to laugh, and to clap,
To wiggle around in excitement
As popcorn spills in my lap!

I always go to the circus
To hear the lions roar,
To see the elephants stand on two feet,
And then to clap for more!

Follow letters from A to Z
And find a friend for you and me!

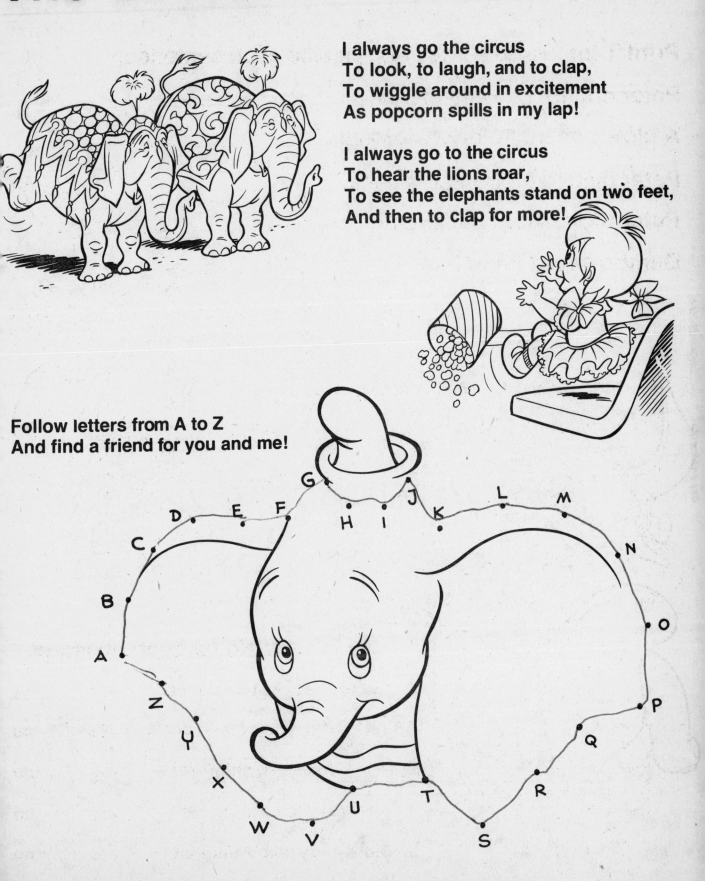

Ten Little Chipmunks

Ten little chipmunks, eating in a line,
One fell asleep, and then there were nine.

Nine little chipmunks, coming in late,
One was missing, and the there was eight.

Eight little chipmunks, counting to eleven,
One couldn't count, and then there were seven.

Seven little chipmunks, making yellow bricks,
One fell down, and then there were six.

Six little chipmunks, learning how to drive,
One hit a rock, and then there were five.

Five little chipmunks, going to the store,
One got lost, and then there were four.

Four little chipmunks, rowing out to sea,
One swam back, and then there were three.

Three little chipmunks, squeezing in a shoe,
One didn't fit, and then there were two.

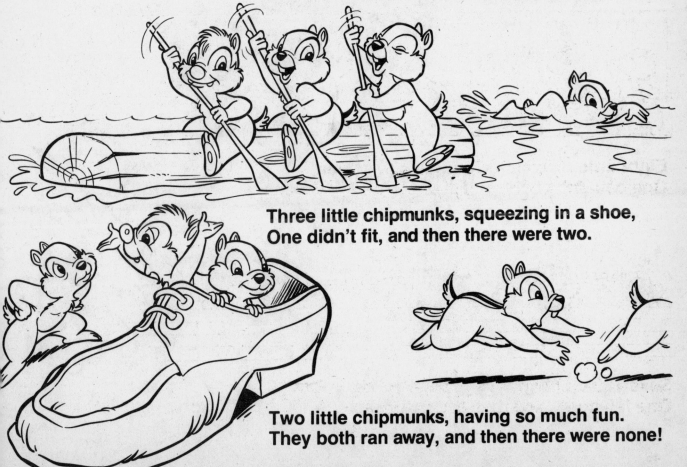

Two little chipmunks, having so much fun.
They both ran away, and then there were none!

Now Do This!

(Circle) the right answer for **each sentence.**

1. How many chipmunks were in a line?   seven   ten

2. Who came in late?   chipmunks   chickens

3. What did the chipmunks count to?   eight   eleven

4. What color were the bricks?   green   yellow

5. What did a chipmunk hit?   rock   sock

6. What did a chipmunk do?   sing   swim

Draw lines to match the rhyming words.

line	eight
late	none
store	three
sea	shoe
two	four
fun	nine

Pick a Poem

City Wheels

The wheels of a city
Make everything go,
From bikes on the sidewalks
To cars in the snow,
Like moving stairs up
And moving stairs down,
The wheels of a city
Go all over town.

Draw a picture of something that has wheels.

A Surprise for Goofy!

Goofy had a job at the circus. It was a good job. He knew he could do it well, even though it was his first time.

"Hot dogs! Ice cream! Popcorn! Peanuts!" called Goofy, as he walked around. He had on a white cape, a white apron with pockets, and he was carrying a big box around his neck. The box held all the food.

"Over here!" called a man. Goofy ran over. "I'll have a hot dog with lots of mustard," said the man.

"Yes, sir," gulped Goofy. "Coming right up, sir." Goofy put the hot dog in the roll. Then he started to squeeze the mustard on. Nothing came out. Goofy squeezed harder. Suddenly the mustard came out in a big rush, squirting all over the man! He was covered with mustard from head to toe.

"Go away!" shouted the man. "Go away!"

Goofy walked on, calling, "Ice cream! Popcorn! Peanuts! Soda pop!"

"Over here," called a lady. "I'll have a can of soda pop. Give me orange."

"Yes, ma'am," gulped Goofy. "Coming right up!" He started to pull the tab on the can. Oooops! The orange soda sprayed up right out of the can. It rained orange pop all over the lady and her friends!

"Go away!" they all shouted. They were really angry at Goofy. "Go away and don't come back!" they shouted.

Poor Goofy. He walked away, calling, "Ice cream! Popcorn! Peanuts!" He hadn't sold one thing yet. And the

Circus was about to begin.

"Over here," called a little boy. Goofy ran over. Nothing was going to go wrong this time. "I'll have a big bag of peanuts," said the little boy.

"Yes, sir!" gulped Goofy. "Coming right up, sir." Goofy took one of his biggest bags from the box. Just as he was about to hand it to the boy, the bag ripped. The peanuts flew down the stairs right to the circus ring! Goofy ran after the peanuts.

Ooooops! Goofy's feet slid on one peanut, another peanut, and another. And Goofy went tumbling right down the stairs! He tumbled over and over— right into the ring! Plop! Splash! He ended up with his head in a water bucket. Goofy sat up. The bucket was on his head. And water was running down all over him!

Poor Goofy! He hung his head. He had goofed again. But what was that? Surprise! The audience was laughing and clapping. They were shouting, "Hurray for Goofy! He's the best clown in the circus."

The circus owner came over to Goofy. "You're fired!" he said. Goofy hung his head again. "You're fired as a food seller. But you're hired as a new clown!"

Now Goofy can goof all he wants in the circus. No one ever tells him to go away. They laugh and laugh and love Goofy, as a circus clown! Goofy has found something he could do better than anyone else!

Now Do This!

Use words from the story to finish each sentence correctly.

Goofy had a job at the _____

Goofy had on a white _____

The man was covered with _____

It rained orange _____

The little boy wanted a bag of _____

Goofy tumbled into the _____

Goofy is the best _____ in the circus.

Circle animals you might find in a circus.

elephants	alligators
bears	horses
cows	skunks
lions	dogs
tigers	snakes

Pick a Poem

Listen! Listen!

Listen to the rain
Going drip, drip, drip.
Listen to the scissors
As they snip, snip, snip.

Listen to a bell
That is tied to a cow.
Listen to the sounds
That you hear right now.

Listen to a bird
Singing high in a tree.
Listen to yourself,
And listen to me!

Circle parts of rhyming words used in the poem.

rain	bell	snip	jar
drip	wish	now	tell
cow	car	pain	me
tree			dish

Thumper Finds a Friend

"Thumper's in a bad mood," sai
Bambi. "That crazy rabbit won't talk t
anybody, not even me."

"What's wrong?" asked Flowe
"Why is Thumper in such a ba
mood?"

"Something is wrong with him,
answered Bambi. "But nobody know
what it is."

Bambi and Flower just didn't kno
what to do to help Thumper. How coul
they help if he wouldn't talk to them?

Suddenly Bambi had a though
"Maybe, just maybe, Thumper will tal
to Jiminy Cricket," said Bambi. "Some
times it's easier to talk to a strange
than a friend. It's hard to tell friend
your problems. Let's ask Jiminy t
help."

"I'll try," said Jiminy when the
asked him. "But Thumper may no
want to talk to me, either."

Jiminy found Thumper sitting unde
a big tree. "Hello, Thumper," he said
"I'm Jiminy Cricket. I'm new aroun
here and I'd like to be friends."

"I'm Thumper," answered the rabbi
"And I'm not in a good mood today. I'r
not in a mood to make friends."

"What's wrong?" asked the cricke
"Maybe I can help you."

Thumper looked down. At last he spoke. "I—I—I can't jump any more," he said. "I can run and I can walk. But I just can't jump. My jumper must be broken."

Jiminy grinned. "I can fix that," he said. "At least, I think I can. Put this collar around your neck."

Thumper did as he was told, but he didn't know how a collar could make him jump again.

Suddenly he did start to jump. He jumped and jumped and jumped! He jumped all over the place! Thumper was so happy he jumped higher than he had ever jumped before.

Jiminy smiled. "See, I told you I could help," grinned the cricket. "There's a secret in the collar you're wearing. It's filled with beans. They're helping you to jump."

"How can beans help?" asked Thumper when he stopped to rest at last.

"They're Mexican jumping beans," said the happy cricket. And he went to tell Bambi and Flower the good news.

Thumper was in a good mood now. His jumper was working again. And best of all, he had found a new friend.

Now Do This!

Print T for True and F for False beside each sentence about the story.

Thumper was in a bad mood. _____

Bambi talked to Flower. _____

Jiminy said he would try to help. _____

Jiminy found Thumper swimming. _____

Jiminy gave Thumper a collar. _____

Thumper jumped very high. _____

Draw lines to match words that go together.

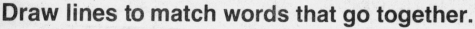

Jiminy   tree

bad   mood

new   Cricket

big   beans

jumping   friend

Write in the missing words. Use words from the
tory about Thumper.

Thumper was in a bad _____. The crazy rabbit

vould not talk to _____. Bambi and Flower wanted

o help _____. They asked Jiminy to _____

o Thumper.

Jiminy gave Thumper a _____. It helped Thumper

o _____ again. Thumper was in a _____

nood now. And he had found a new _____.

**Fix the mixed-up words. Write them
on the lines.**

ambiB   _____

tibrab   _____

ctrkice   _____

wolreF   _____

pmTheru   _____

Pick a Poem

I Never Met a Crocodile

I've never met a crocodile,
Nor taken one to lunch,
But if I did, I wonder what
The croc would like to munch.

I've never met a crocodile,
Nor ever heard one roar,
But if I did, I wonder if
I'd rather hear it snore!

I've never met a crocodile,
And hope I never do,
But if that day should ever come,
I'd not shake hands—would you

Now Do This!

Follow the crocodile's path. Find where it is going.

What would **you** do if **you** met a crocodile?

_____

_____

_____

_____

_____

The Magic Hour

Gray and Black were cats. But they were not real cats. They were cat bookends. They sat back-to-back all day long. They held up books on a high shelf.

One night, at the magic hour of twelve, Gray and Black came alive. "I'm tired of holding up books," said Gray. "I want to see the world."

"So do I," said Black. "I'm with you! Let's get down off this shelf and see the great big world."

"Look, here's a roller skate," said Gray. "Let's go for a ride."

So Gray and Black rode around on the roller skate. They saw Cleo swimming in a bowl. They saw Scamp chewing a bone. They saw Casey, Jr. running on his little track. They even saw Cinderella sitting by the fire! "Wheee!" shouted Gray and Black. "Isn't the world great?"

"Bong!" went the big old clock. The magic hour was over. "Time to hold up books again," said Gray.

The two cats jumped back up to the high shelf. "Uh-oh!" said Gray. "Look at our books. They all fell over."

"I know what to do," said Black. "You sit down near the books and I'll push."

Gray sat down and Black pushed hard. Up, up went the books. Then Black sat down, too. The two cats were bookends once again. But now they were happy bookends. They had seen the world at last!

Now Do This!

(Circle) the sentence that tells something about Gray and Black.

Gray and Black are cats.

Bookends are good ducks.

Gray wants to see the world.

The magic hour is twelve.

Gray and Black see Dumbo.

Gray and Black see the world.

What does each word mean? Write the number of each word on the correct line.

1. bookends _____ a place to put things

2. magic _____ things that hold up books

3. shelf _____ to use your teeth to eat

4. chew _____ the earth

5. world _____ a special power

Our Puppy

We have a friendly puppy
With a warm and wiggly nose,
He's always poking into things,
No matter where he goes.
He's always into mischief,
When he chews, or bumps a lamp,
So though we love him very much,
We had to name him Scamp!

The End

Sherrie Marie walter
Ricky water

Walter Family

Richard walter

Jackie E. walter

Sherrie Marie walter

Richard dail walter